IMAGES
of America

Los Angeles
Police Department

*Over the past 150 years, the hard work and
dedication of thousands of police officers has
resulted in the unparalleled reputation of the Los
Angeles Police Department. Today's officers and
those who will take their places in the future are
deeply indebted to those who forged that image.
The Los Angeles Police Historical Society is
committed to preserving and telling the story of
this fine department, and dedicates this book to
all officers, especially those officers who have
made the ultimate sacrifice, as well as civilian
members of the department and members of
the community who have contributed to this
legendary legacy.*

ON THE COVER: The motorcycle squad enjoys a visit from cowboy film star Ken Maynard sometime
during the early 1930s at an inspection held at the Griffith Park Riding Academy. It only seemed
fair, since one of the squad wanted his photo taken astride Ken's horse, Tarzan, that the famous
movie cowboy try out one of LAPD's "mechanical steeds."

IMAGES
of America

LOS ANGELES
POLICE DEPARTMENT

Thomas G. Hays and Arthur W. Sjoquist
Los Angeles Police Historical Society

Foreword by Chief William J. Bratton

ARCADIA

ISBN 0-7385-3025-5

Published by Arcadia Publishing
Charleston SC, Chicago IL, Portsmouth NH, San Francisco CA

Printed in Great Britain

Library of Congress Catalog Card Number: 2005927047

For all general information contact Arcadia Publishing at:
Telephone 843-853-2070
Fax 843-853-0044
E-mail sales@arcadiapublishing.com
For customer service and orders:
Toll-Free 1-888-313-2665
Visit us on the Internet at www.arcadiapublishing.com

ACKNOWLEDGMENTS

Researching and working on this book has been a rewarding experience that has brought us closer to the many fine men and women of the Los Angeles Police Department who have gone before us. They have given their blood, sweat, tears, and, in many instances, their lives to make this department one in which we can all be proud.

First and foremost, we want to recognize Lt. John L. Thomas, who, despite working full time, came in to the Los Angeles Police Museum and Community Education Center, got his hands dirty searching through old pictures, did research, wrote captions, and tracked down hard-to-find photographs. His contribution was significant and added greatly to the book.

We also would like to thank the following people for their support and enthusiasm for the project: from the Los Angeles Police Historical Society, executive director Glynn Martin, museum operations manager Pamela Huhane, and outreach coordinator Melinda Hays. We also thank Charlie Diaz of Charlie's Printing Service and Matthew Sjoquist, senior copywriter/editor for Movielink. Additional contributions were made by Marc Wanamaker of Bison Productions, LAPD officer James Ungari, Sgt. Catherine Plows of the LAPD Media Relations Section, Tracey Schuster of the Getty Research Institute, curator of photographs Carolyn Kozo Cole of the Los Angeles Public Library, and LAPD public information officer Mary Grady.

Finally, special thanks must go to Claudia Diaz, administrative manager of the Los Angeles Police Historical Society, without whose help there would be no book. Claudia, in addition to her regular duties, coordinated the scanning and final assembly of the book. In stark contrast to the authors' computer ignorance, her technical knowledge and support were critical and played a key role in the development of this book.

The Los Angeles Police Historical Society authorized this project, and, unless otherwise noted, all photographs in this book are from the archives of the Los Angeles Police Museum and Community Education Center.

**The Los Angeles Police Department™ and LAPD™
are registered trademarks of the City of Los Angeles.**

CONTENTS

FOREWORD

In 2004, I wrote the foreword for *Scene of the Crime*, a book about the Los Angeles Police Department that is quite different from the one you are about to read. It was a historical collection of gritty crime scene (mostly homicide) photographs that required me to warn the reader that they were about to be exposed to a graphic, sometimes depressing, sordid side of police work.

This book offers a different perspective. Although it is also a pictorial review of the LAPD, it takes a more balanced approach in its depiction of the police officer's job. While the grim, violent side of police work will always be there, it is important to know that there is much more to being a police officer. Of course, you will learn a little about the history of the LAPD, but you will also be privy to the excitement, danger, comedy, heartbreak, and complexity of being a police officer.

What kind of person chooses to do police work? Or even better, why do they do it? The pay is barely adequate, and sometimes after officers have done the best job they can, they are criticized, investigated, sued, fired—and even prosecuted. So why indeed do they do it?

Police officers are just regular people, but in some ways they are unique. They want to spend their lives doing something that can make other people's lives better. They see themselves as the "good guys"—the ones wearing the white hats who ride to the rescue when good people need help. They are the ones who defy logic and survival instincts, and run *toward* the gunfire instead of away from it. They know that often times on the other side of that thin blue line is anarchy and chaos. Police officers believe they can make a difference. Making a difference in Los Angeles can be one of the most daunting challenges in American policing.

The LAPD is one of the most understaffed police departments in the world (a force that is only half the size of what it should be to police Los Angeles), and thus the Los Angeles police officer has had to evolve into a multitalented, flexible problem-solver. He or she must be capable of dealing with an array of situations without the backup assistance that is so common in other cities' departments. In the sprawling metropolis of Los Angeles, police officers are spread thinly. If an officer gets into trouble, backup is likely not around the corner and probably a long time coming.

This challenge, coupled with the LAPD's fierce dedication to providing impeccable protection and service, means the Los Angeles police officer has to utilize a uniquely proactive style of police work. Despite the overwhelming odds (and sometimes underwhelming public support), the LAPD has managed to actually lower the crime rate 16 percent in the last two years.

I've been privileged to be appointed commissioner of both the Boston and New York Police Departments and to work with many fine dedicated officers. But for almost three years I have served as the chief of the Los Angeles Police Department, and this has been an experience like no other.

Los Angeles police officers, both retired and active, firmly believe they are members of the finest police force in the world. Much like the United States Marine Corps, they feel they are the best and are willing to defend that reputation to their last breath. They are unquestionably second to none.

Credit for this success can only be attributed to the outstanding quality and dedication of the individual Los Angeles police officer. For over 50 years, the LAPD has been committed to the goal of honest, corruption-free, proactive police work. On occasion, there have been lapses by individual members of the department. Nonetheless, the department and the overwhelming majority of its personnel have remained true to that goal. I hope this book will not only give you some insight into a police officer's job, but also a glimpse of the pride and esprit de corps that created the world-famous legacy of the Los Angeles police officer. I hope you enjoy it.

—Chief of Police William J. Bratton
Los Angeles, California, 2005

INTRODUCTION

The Los Angeles Police Department is the most praised, criticized, and misunderstood police department in the world—yet it is also the most imitated. Why? The answer lies in its evolution from one of the nation's most corrupt law enforcement agencies to the most advanced and professional police department in the world—an odyssey from posses to professionals. That story, stretching back over 150 years, is both grim and inspiring, a journey replete with politics, corruption, bravery, and dedication, inextricably entwined with the history of the City of Los Angeles itself. This book is a brief tribute to the men and women behind the LAPD badge who have faithfully served their city.

The story of the LAPD begins in 1850 with the establishment of California as the 31st state and the incorporation of the City of Los Angeles. The first formal law enforcement consisted of a lone city marshal whose duties included tax collection and licensing saloons and legally operating brothels. With the California gold rush beckoning hordes of fortune seekers westward, Los Angeles was soon seething with shootings, gambling, and carousing desperadoes. As a result, in June 1853, the Common Council of Los Angeles authorized a police force of 100 volunteers. These men, the first police officers, wore white ribbon badges bearing the words "City Police—Authorized by the Council of Los Angeles" in both English and Spanish. Dr. A. W. Hope served as chief of the group, which became known as the Los Angeles Rangers.

It was not until 1869 that the police force evolved from a voluntary organization to a paid city department. William C. Warren, the new city marshal (and grandfather of legendary sheriff Eugene Biscailuz), commanded a force of six men working in two shifts about six days a week. In lieu of salaries, the officers' compensation depended on the fees they collected in the city, which now boasted a population of nearly 5,000. The last city marshal was Juan J. Carrillo. Then, in 1876, the city council eliminated the office of city marshal and appointed ex-councilman Jacob F. Gerkins as the first chief of police of Los Angeles.

Although the population of Los Angeles soared to nearly 50,000 during the boom days of the 1880s, the meager police force grew to only 31 officers. But things changed in 1889 with the appointment of the first truly notable figure to oversee Los Angeles law enforcement: Chief John M. Glass, who is credited with the first organizational development of the LAPD. He also implemented the first timekeeping system and the first systematic supervision of personnel by dividing the city into four police districts. By this method, the sergeants—or "roundsmen"—could more capably monitor their patrolmen's beats.

Around the same time, patrolmen adopted a military appearance with the acquisition of 45 to 70 Winchester rifles. With the department conducting regular drills on a vacant lot at Second and Broadway and the men adorned with semi-military hats and brass-buttoned uniforms, the "new" LAPD officers became known as the "Pride of the State."

Chief Glass fought continuously for better equipment and pay and helped secure service and disability pensions for his men. Believing that discipline was implicit to morale and efficiency, he conducted frequent inspections astride his beloved white horse.

The colorful period of history that was Chief Glass's regime saw many more "firsts"—standards that today seem fundamental but exist only due to Glass's fearless vision and leadership. The city constructed Central Station and started operation of a records bureau, with California's first-ever adoption of the Bertillon system of identification. Other innovations included the first police matron, the first patrol wagon, the first substation (Boyle Heights, now Hollenbeck), the first alarm system (Gamewell), and the first entry-level standards for new offices.

By the turn of the century, Los Angeles's population of 102,000 dwarfed the department's force of only 69 men. As always, the city's prosperity also brought new problems. Chief Glass discovered that his department was neither equipped nor trained to handle Los Angeles traffic jams, not to mention the increased violent crime. New political pressures also surfaced as one of the chief's major challenges, including unionism, labor strikes, and big business. In the early

1900s, mayors preferred to appoint an "outsider" as chief, enabling them to not only control the police department but also to implement their policies with little interference. Consequently, between 1900 and 1923, 16 different chiefs held office.

A bright spot came in 1923, when August Vollmer, chief of police of Berkeley, California, and a criminology expert, agreed to take over the LAPD for one year. Vollmer promptly inaugurated new methods of organization, including scientific methods of detection, administration, and selection and training of officers. After one year of service, Vollmer resigned as chief, but his operational theories and changes were accepted and continued.

In 1933, another period of corruption came under the iron fist of Mayor Frank L. Shaw and his brother Joe, who used the police and fire departments for their own personal gain. City contracts were bought and sold, while bribery and corruption became the norm. Even police promotions were sold for the right price

Reform took hold again in 1938, when Mayor Fletcher Bowron, a former judge, took office and made the cleanup of city government his primary goal. Within the next six months, 45 high-ranking police officers had resigned. To this day, no criminal or politically corrupt group has ever again controlled the LAPD.

In 1949, the board of police commissioners appointed retired Marine Corps general William A. Worton as interim chief. With military vigor, Worton shuffled personnel, rewarding the good and disciplining the bad and, in effect, restoring morale. Along with a series of strategic innovations, Worton introduced a military-style intelligence squad to scout the underworld and keep abreast of mobsters' plans.

In 1950, the most historically profound era of the LAPD began with the appointment of William H. Parker as the chief of police. Parker, who had become a police officer in 1927 while studying law, would go on to serve for 16 years—the longest tenure in the department's history. His revolutionary standards of professionalism still resonate throughout the LAPD to this day. Parker's service as chief under three different Los Angeles mayors attests to his integrity and freedom from political control. In his first year, Parker made sweeping changes to all levels of the department, modernizing management and improving efficiency. His innovative policy of using qualified civilians to do administrative work freed 108 officers to return to patrol duties, keeping the city safe.

Parker's influence extended far beyond local communities. He received worldwide recognition for his accomplishments in law enforcement and even made history in the civil rights struggle. In the early 1960s, Parker initiated department-wide racial integration. Prior to that time, black officers only worked in black areas with black partners. Parker's bulldog determination and unquestioned authority enabled him to shatter racial barriers in a time when such a thing was both unheard of and considered impossible by most police officials.

In 1966, Chief Parker died of a heart attack during an engagement as a guest speaker at a military banquet. Parker's death ended an era—possibly the most productive and renowned in the history of American municipal law enforcement. He left a tradition to be upheld by all future Los Angeles police officers and an everlasting example for other police agencies to follow.

In 1967, Deputy Chief Thomas Reddin took over as chief of police. He served for only two years before he made a surprise announcement: he was resigning to take a position as a newscaster for a local television station.

Chief Reddin was followed by Chief Edward M. Davis, the 46th man to hold the post. Chief Davis was one of the department's more flamboyant and outspoken chiefs, frequently quoted in the news media for various "outrageous" statements. A strong, no-nonsense chief, he once confided that to be a good chief in Los Angeles, "you had to be a tough son of a bitch."

Chief Davis, among many other innovations, implemented the Basic Car Plan concept, bringing the police officer and the citizen closer together. After a distinguished career, Chief Davis retired from the department in January 1978, and then won a seat in the state senate.

In March 1978, Daryl F. Gates, a 29-year veteran of the LAPD, became chief of police after participating in a unique examination process. For the first time, the vacant chief's position had been opened up to executive-level police personnel across the nation. Chief Gates, who had once been Chief Parker's driver and adjutant, took over the department during a period of declining personnel and equipment. The city's population was nearly three million and there were less than two officers per 1,000 persons, one of the lowest ratios of any other major city police department in the United States.

Chief Gates also implemented the now famous DARE program, designed to teach elementary school children to avoid drugs and eventually adopted worldwide. Chief Gates also took great pride in the outstanding performance of SWAT and was the recognized champion of that concept.

In 1991, the LAPD and the City of Los Angeles were rocked by the Rodney King incident and the ensuing riots. These events caused the leaders of the city to closely scrutinize department policies and training methods. That led to a change of leadership in mid-1992 when Willie L. Williams was appointed chief of police.

Chief Williams, who had served as the police commissioner of Philadelphia, was the first "outsider" at the helm of the LAPD since the 1940s. Chief Williams served for a fixed term of five years and was replaced by 32-year LAPD veteran Bernard C. Parks. Chief Parks succeeded in cutting significant layers of bureaucracy, introducing new systems of accountability, and moving rapidly toward his vision of community government. In early 2002, in the midst of the implementation of a Federal Consent Decree to change some department practices, the city declined to grant Chief Parks a second five-year term.

In October 2002, William J. Bratton, former commissioner of the New York and Boston Police Departments, became the 54th chief of police. It was not long before Chief Bratton realized the dilemma faced by every previous Los Angeles chief of police since 1870—the department is severely understaffed! Because officers are spread so thinly in this sprawling metropolis of 460 square miles, Chief Bratton has gone on record saying that Los Angeles is "the most dangerous place to be a police officer." In response to the challenge, Chief Bratton has devised several innovative strategies to put more officers in the field.

Over 150 years of history have been told sparsely here due to time and space. Today the question asked is, "What does the future hold?" The rapid and sometimes unwelcome changes of the recent past worry many, and the future seems uncertain. But the department continues to hire and train high-quality officers. Men and women who are prepared to serve even beyond the call of duty continue to be well represented in the ranks of the Los Angeles Police Department.

The LAPD badge has evolved over the years.

Badge No. 1	1869–1890
Badge No. 2	1890–1909
Badge No. 3	1909–1913
Badge No. 4	1913–1923
Badge No. 5	1923–1940
Badge No. 6	1940–2005

One

THE WILD WEST

1890–1900

The plaza area around a church is depicted in downtown Los Angeles, *c.* 1869, the same year the first paid police department, consisting of six officers, was formed.

The Chinese Massacre occurred on this infamous street, Calle De Los Negros, or "Nigger Alley," as it was sadly known in 1871. The block, located at Aliso Street where Los Angeles Street now crosses the freeway, was made up mostly of saloons and brothels. Reputedly at least one murder a day occurred here. Living on the street were mostly Chinese people, 19 of whom were hanged nearby during the massacre in October 1871. In 1877, the block was torn down and renamed Los Angeles Street. Parker Center and the federal building are located there today.

After serving as the last-ever city marshal in 1876, Juan Carrillo went on to become mayor of Santa Monica and Santa Barbara. Carrillo was the father of actor Leo Carrillo, who played Pancho in the TV series *The Cisco Kid*. In 1877, the Office of the Chief of Police was established. In those days, foot patrolmen earned $90 per month, and mounted officers an additional $5. The city marshal received only $10 more.

In 1876, members of the LAPD began wearing regulation uniforms that featured an "old frontier" felt hat and a knee-length blue serge coat. The eight-pointed silver star, considered quite elegant, was purchased by the patrolmen at a cost of $6. The duties of police officers included enforcing laws that prohibited opium sales and cattle grazing or herding in the streets and regulating the six-mile-per-hour speed limit of steam trains within city limits. Officers also had to pick up loose paper blown about in the streets, lest it spook the horses.

Chief Emil Harris (December 27, 1877–December 5, 1878) was the second chief of police for Los Angeles and the only Jewish chief. As an officer, he helped to rescue Chinese victims from lynch mobs during the Chinese Massacre of October 1871.

The entire Los Angeles Police Department gathers at the L.A. County courthouse on Broadway south of Temple Street, c. 1890. Lucy Gray and her daughter Aletha Gilbert, the city's first "City Mother," are in the front row. The Detective Bureau is in civilian clothes. In 1888, Lucy Thompson Gray was appointed the city's first Matron. Mrs. Gray, who lived near the women's jail with her 10 children, had adopted the custom of also caring for homeless youngsters. In 1896, a new jail with a women's section was constructed on First Street. The complex included adjacent living quarters for the Matron, who lived there 24 hours a day, visiting home only occasionally. Mrs. Gray was also the nurse for female patients at Central Receiving Hospital in the same building. She even helped detectives with difficult cases. Mrs. Gray was a pioneer woman, imbued with independence, determination, and compassion, despite her slight stature. Four years before her death, her fellow officers presented her with a gold badge. She worked until four days before her death in February 1904, from pneumonia.

The Strongmen Team (*c.* 1889) was a group of early LAPD officers who competed in weight lifting, wrestling, bare-knuckle boxing, and other "feats of strength" against "all challengers." In the early years of the department, physical strength was the primary qualification for becoming a police officer. One of the team's members was Robert William Stewart, the LAPD's first African American officer. Joining the department in 1886, Stewart's extraordinary size (six feet, four inches; 240 pounds) made him well suited for police work in early Los Angeles.

LAPD officers wearing the original fedora-style hat line up for inspection, *c.* 1880.

While this photograph from the archives is quaint and provides a peek into a police department office of the 1890s, what the officer sitting at the incredibly cluttered desk is saying to the man wearing the visor will never be known. Presumably it's not an admonishment about neatness!

This *c.* 1900 photograph of an officer astride his horse shows him wearing the second badge in a series of six that the Los Angeles Police Department has worn through the years (see page 10). The current and most famous design was adopted in 1940. Just so everybody would know that he also is a member of LAPD, the officer's "partner" sports the same badge on his bridle.

In this highly dramatic shot taken around 1895, a Los Angeles police officer surveys a very busy fire department crew as they fire up their horse-drawn steam boilers to attain and keep maximum hose pressure in order to do their job.

In 1889, helmeted officers stand for their portrait on the steps of the new city hall on Broadway. They are wearing the "sunburst" style badge, which was the first LAPD badge design.

A mounted contingent of LAPD officers takes to the street in this turn-of-the-century photograph. From the size of the crowd and the floral neckpiece on the lead horse, this is probably the annual La Fiesta Parade, which was created in 1894 as a sort of tourist attraction to lure visitors to the city. This Spanish-themed event occurred annually for over 40 years.

In 1896, horsepower along with footpower were the two means of response to calls for service. The main stable for the department was located in the basement of the main police station at First and Hill Streets. Note the very early double-wired electric lights—undoubtedly a significant improvement for a normally dark, below-ground area.

This unusual-looking patrol vehicle was electric and was acquired by the LAPD around the turn of the 20th century, when this picture was taken. When delivering prisoners to the jail, the patrol wagon would head in towards the jail door and park. A turntable (visible in the pavement) would then turn the wagon around allowing arrestees to exit directly into the building, minimizing the chance for escape. The wagon was then ready to take to the streets again without further maneuvering.

Chief John M. Glass's 11-year tenure as chief (1889–1900) remained the longest for more than 50 years. He formed the first Detective Bureau and also imposed military-style efficiency on the department, equipping his patrolmen with snappy uniforms and 45 to 70 Winchester rifles. Under his leadership, the department soon became known as the "Pride of the State."

Another large turnout of officers prepares for an inspection (and obligatory photograph) on a sunny residential street at the turn of the 20th century. Knowing those uniforms were made of wool and what the summers are like in this city, hopefully the inspection was mercifully brief.

In 1889, Chief John Glass is seated on the right with the first Detective Bureau.

In this photograph at the dawn of the 20th century, helmeted LAPD officers are directly down in front as Pres. William McKinley reviews an annual La Fiesta Parade from under the flag-draped canopy of an elaborate reviewing stand.

An impressive white-gloved group of L.A.'s finest stands at attention for their photograph sometime around the turn of the 20th century. If one looks closely, it appears that the mounted unit passed by just before this shot was made.

Two

PRIDE OF THE STATE

1900–1920

This photograph was identified only as the Annual Police Inspection on May 1, 1912. For many years, the inspection concluded with a public parade, which is most likely what happened here. Sergeant Toolen leads the group, assisted by Sergeant Hoover, at far right in the first rank, as they step out smartly at Eighth and Spring Streets in the heart of downtown.

Sgt. Julian Ingersoll Peterson, who was upgraded in rank in September 1904, poses for a formal portrait upon being promoted. Note the six-pointed badge reproduced under his sergeant stripes.

The first University Police Substation in 1905 provides a backdrop for an early automobile police patrol, probably an "Oakland" model. The driver is Officer Frank Shriner with Captain Bradish.

A trough of flash powder illuminates these officers in a group shot taken in 1907, probably at Central Station. It's interesting to observe the coexistence of gas and electric fixtures over their heads, indicating that the new electric lights may not have been completely reliable yet. Someone should have thought to remove the spittoon prior to the shutter being snapped, but then those things were definitely part of the workplace at the turn of the century.

Although this early 1900s officer may appear to be taking a "break," we are sure he would simply claim to be doing "undercover" work.

In 1903, the Gamewell Company installed a private telephone system for the LAPD. Simple as it may seem by today's standards, the system was a major step in communicating with officers on the beat. Previously, officers had to go to the station to pick up assignments or, in some cases, a runner was sent out to find them. Special squads of officers were kept at the station to respond to emergencies. This new system allowed officers to check in at intervals from phone boxes on street corners and enabled them to check out suspects without taking them to the station. A switchboard was located at the station to enable the calls to be transferred to the detectives, a supervisor, the records unit, etc. An updated version of this system was in use well into the middle of the century, and later replaced by dial telephones in the boxes. With the advent of hand-held radios, cell phones, etc., the call box system was abandoned. The photograph shows the original department switchboard and four officers discussing the new technology.

Three LAPD officers proudly pose with their horses and patrol wagon in 1908.

The Bicycle Squad, shown in this action photograph from the early 1900s, was first implemented under Chief John Glass.

Maybe "It Never Rains in Southern California," as the song goes, but in 1907 Officer L. S. Amman modeled the latest rain slicker just in case. One wonders if the California pennant was there as an inside joke.

In November 1906, Walter H. Auble (November 1, 1905–November 20, 1906) was replaced as chief of police and returned to his permanent position as captain of detectives. On the morning of September 9, 1908, he and Capt. Paul E. Flammer learned that a burglary was being planned. They followed the suspects and decided to make an arrest rather than wait until the burglary occurred. The suspects struggled with the officers and shot Auble with his own gun. The killer escaped but was later tracked down and arrested with the assistance of many law enforcement agencies and over 100 citizen volunteers. As the suspect was being taken into custody, he swallowed potassium cyanide and died within the hour. Captain Auble became the third Los Angeles police officer to be killed in the line of duty. Since he had served as the interim chief, Auble remains the highest-ranking officer to have given his life in the line of duty.

In this 1907 photograph of Officer Oren L. Poor, he wears the second-series badge, the helmet style headgear worn until around 1910, and a finely turned nightstick. It appears one of his offspring thought to make the observation at the bottom of the photograph, as Poor had a lengthy career, retiring as a captain in 1928.

" Pop when he was young "

LAPD supervisors pause for this 1906 photograph. Chief Walter H. Auble is on the far right.

In 1909, several officers and two horses assigned to the harbor area pose for their picture in San Pedro.

The ruins of the *Los Angeles Times* building still smolder after the McNamara brothers blew it up during a 1910 labor dispute, killing 21 *Times* employees. The brothers were captured and stood trial in Los Angeles, defended by the famous trial attorney Clarence Darrow. This is one of the few cases Darrow lost.

Chief of Police Alexander Galloway relaxes in his office, *c.* 1910. Chief Galloway had never been a police officer and was completely inexperienced when he was appointed by the local politicians. His term in office lasted a brief ten months.

Since 1886, African American officers have proudly served the City of Los Angeles as police officers. These early uniformed pioneers (c. 1912), from left to right, are (seated) Patrolmen Littleton McDuff and William Glenn; (standing) Frank White, William Stevens, and Allen Watson. Throughout much of the department's history, black officers were subjected to racial discrimination. They were prohibited from working with non-black partners, excluded from working outside the city's black community, and denied equal promotional opportunities. Today black officers have equal opportunities and have advanced to every rank and assignment within the department. To date, the LAPD has had two black chiefs of police.

This splendid, c. 1907 photograph reveals one of the first motorized police vehicles—believed to be an Oakland. Note the pre-1909 badge emblem on the rear door. The undersized letters "LAPD" barely whisper the vehicle's identity.

In 1910, Alice Stebbins Wells was sworn in as the LAPD's and the nation's first policewoman. Mrs. Wells had a background in theology and social work and saw a need for women in "modern" police work. She later received Policewoman's Badge No. 1. A charismatic speaker, she toured the United States and Canada promoting the cause of female officers, resulting in the appointment of policewomen in many of the cities she visited. Her travels were not compensated by the city and were all on leaves of absence. In 1915, Wells founded—and was the first president of—the International Association of Police Women. In 1928, she cofounded the Women Peace Officers Association of California and was elected its first president.

A fine-looking group of Los Angeles police officers pose for the camera sometime around 1917–1918 to record the fact that they worked the Hollenbeck Division, policing the eastern part of the city. The old station, built in 1912 and razed in 1964, stands as a backdrop. Hollenbeck was built in the Boyle Heights section of the city and was the department's first substation.

Members of the "Speed Squad" show off their new Indian motorcycles in front of the old Goodyear plant, c. 1913.

Shown here in front of the old Central Station at First and Hill Streets in 1913 are three "Oaklands," part of the LAPD's first motorized patrol. Central Station, the department headquarters, was opened in 1896 and demolished in 1955, when Parker Center opened.

A group of well-groomed officers gather for a photograph about 1912, holding their relatively new round police hats in front of them. Just the year before, the department changed from the old-style, cloth-covered helmets.

Some University Division officers pause to show off their motor cars and bikes on Jefferson Boulevard in 1914, halting a streetcar in the process.

John Butler was chief of police during World War I and is shown at the end of the table, flanked by his staff. The development of the department suffered a temporary lull, since most city activities were devoted to the war. Butler formed a "War Squad" to deal with the many offenders of the Espionage Act and other war acts. In its first three months of operation, the squad made 220 arrests for antiwar activities, including "Seditious Utterances," "Failure to Register as a German Alien Enemy," and worse, for being a "Suspicious Alien Enemy." On the wall is a photograph of the previous chief, Charles E. Sebastian (1911–1915). Chief Sebastian, having established a solid reputation for his crusade against vice, used his popularity with the conservative community to run for mayor. During the campaign, Sebastian was accused and brought to trial on a morals charge. After a witness in the case admitted to perjury, a relieved public sent the popular chief to city hall. Sebastian was the first police officer to be elected mayor.

This photograph, taken outside the old police headquarters building at First and Hill Streets prior to 1920, would seem to reflect the lure of the uniform on the ladies. The sparse note on the photograph merely indicates that the ladies are "screenstars." Apparently the rank and file decided to line up behind their boss and try to get their share of attention.

1919 ~ Chaingang taken in Griffith Park
Note balls and chains at feet

This photograph is undeniably fascinating but also a mystery. As noted by its original caption at the top, it depicts a 1919 chain gang at work in Griffith Park. LAPD was assigned sentenced misdemeanor prisoners, called trustees, by the courts to perform various "housekeeping" tasks in stations and jails for several years until the program ended about 1963. Certainly the ball and chain device was never part of that program and the work was not done in Griffith Park. While it makes for an interesting picture in our files, the practice has mercifully disappeared from sentencing policies by the local courts.

Officer E. E. Novgaard and Sgt. J. T. Evert pose for a photograph at their desks in old Hollywood station, ready to grab the candlestick-style telephones between them should a call come in. The three calendars on the wall tell us the year is 1916, and the ever-present spittoon tells us chewing tobacco was popular with the officers.

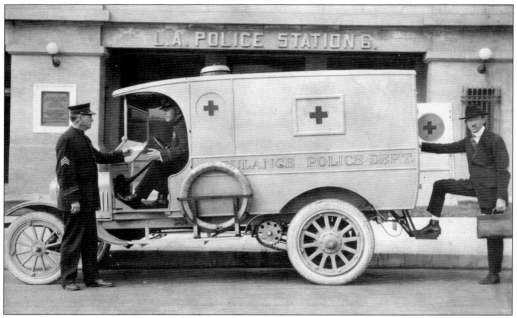

Up until the 1930s, it was not uncommon for fire and police to share buildings in Los Angeles. In this case, Station No. 6 indicates the Hollywood Division and this building, which was located in the 1600 block of North Cahuenga Boulevard, not only was adjacent to the fire department (out of picture on the right), but housed a new Ford Model T police ambulance, as shown in this 1918 photograph. Subsequently the fire department took over the city's emergency ambulance service, which it continues to provide.

In September 1919, Pres. Woodrow Wilson visited Los Angeles to promote the League of Nations. President Wilson suffered a breakdown six days later and, on October 2, 1919, was incapacitated by a stroke.

Three

THREE DECADES OF TUMULT

1920–1950

The WCTU (Women's Christian Temperance Union) with Chief James E. Davis (on the left in the dark suit) pauses while breaking up a distillery during Prohibition, *c.* 1928.

This photograph was taken the day that the 18th Amendment, prohibiting the manufacture, sale, or transportation of alcohol, went into effect, ushering in the Prohibition era. For the next 14 years, until the amendment's repeal in 1933, the LAPD and its Vice Squad would fight a losing battle against bootleggers, racketeers, dishonest judges, crooked politicians, and its own crooked cops. Standing in the front row, third from the left, is James E. Davis, who would work his way to the head of the Vice Squad and eventually the head of the department.

A member of Chief James Davis's world-famous shooting team is apparently well-prepared to carry out the chief's orders concerning gangsters.

Nine of University Division's officers pause in their duties for a photographer to capture them in front of the old station on West Jefferson Boulevard sometime around 1921. The young man in the short pants apparently thought it was a pretty good looking group and decided he wanted to be part of it.

Three uniformed LAPD officers along with a detective check out an illegal still during the challenging years of Prohibition in the Roaring Twenties. While a lot of sheiks and flappers thought of the police as only out to spoil their fun, enforcement was a highly dangerous activity. Not only was the illegal liquor often controlled by professional and violent gangsters, but the stills were also known to explode if not "decommissioned" properly. (Courtesy Security Pacific Collection, Los Angeles Public Library.)

—Vanderbilt Photo

Women of the Los Angeles police department yesterday took part in their first practice shoot at the Elysian Park range.
Photos show:

No. 1. Miss Stella Wallen showing how policewomen should carry firearms.

No. 3. The noise bothers Miss Edith P. Mathes who puts cotton in her ears.

This 1925 photograph layout appeared in *Pacific Police Magazine*. Female police officers have changed a lot since then—not only in their uniforms and duties (as well as dropping the term "policewoman") but also in their numbers and contributions. Opportunities for women are unlimited in today's modern LAPD. Margaret York, the first female deputy chief, recently retired. Sharon Papa the first woman to ascend to the rank of assistant chief, currently serves as the highest-ranking female.

In 1923, Officer Thomas, whose two sons later rose to the rank of lieutenant and captain, stands guard over a promising citation in the event a motorist fails to see the hydrant.

42

An unusual "mobile jail" concept is tested in the field in the late 1920s. One suspects that this experiment was intended to prevent motor officers from having to call patrol cars to help control or transport prisoners.

The "Gun Squad" captures what appears to be a dangerous felon in the 1920s. Working with greatly reduced resources, Chief James E. Davis made vice, radical organizations, and vagrants his primary targets. But the "Eastern Gunman" was the chief's most pressing concern. Since Davis believed that accurate shooting by police was the greatest deterrent to this type of criminal, he formed a 50-member "Gun Squad." He then announced that, "The gun-toting element and the rum smugglers are going to learn that murder and gun toting are most inimical to their best interests. If the courts won't eliminate them [he would]." Davis warned that he would "hold court on gunmen in the Los Angeles streets; I want them [gangsters] brought in dead, not alive." Davis vowed to "reprimand any officer who shows the least mercy to a criminal."

A group of grim-faced detectives exit old Central Station on First Street in the mid-1920s carrying an impressive arsenal en route to a hot call.

Jackie Coogan was a child star in 1923, having made *The Kid* with Charlie Chaplin. He and his family lived in the Wilshire District and he frequently roamed the neighborhood in his midget motor-driven car. Virtually every policeman in the area knew Jackie and made an extra effort to look out for him as this officer is doing. While this photograph smacks of a publicity shot, it does show what kind of a neat toy you get when you're a child movie star. (Courtesy Marc Wanamaker.)

Chief R. Lee Heath purchased 10 Colt semi-automatic 30-06 Army-style rifles to help the department's fight against rum-running, a major problem statewide that had resulted in the shooting of several police officers. These and other military weapons were considered in response to this problem, but were never adopted due to the danger of accidents in a densely crowded city. Chief Heath started with the department in 1904 as a police officer, serving as chief from 1924 to 1926. In 1971, at the age of 92, he was still living in Tujunga, California, with his wife. After retiring from the department he became an attorney. Interviewed for a book on LAPD history, his razor-sharp memory was amazing.

Chief of Police R. Lee Heath is seen here at the Stamford, Connecticut, Colt Arms factory examining a .30 caliber water-cooled machine gun for the department. The weapon was not purchased. Heath was considered the most powerful politician in the department, which grew during his tenure to include construction of five police stations and the introduction of the Photo Lab and Chemical Lab, forerunners of Scientific Investigation Division. Chief Heath also established the first police training school as a separate division, and went on to create the Medal of Valor. The award was first given in 1925 to Sgt. Frank Harper, who was involved in a gun battle with a gangland hoodlum. To this day, it is the highest honor the department can bestow on an officer.

It's pretty clear that, in the early 1920s, this motorcycle officer ticketed a man who had a cart being pulled on a main thoroughfare by an ostrich! The burning question is: What reason could he possibly be giving for doing so? Whatever it was, the officer apparently decided it wasn't good enough to cut him any slack.

Officer John Fowler, who's almost invisible against the stake bed truck, takes his life in his hands directing traffic at Tenth and Main Streets during a fairly substantial rainstorm, *c.* 1925.

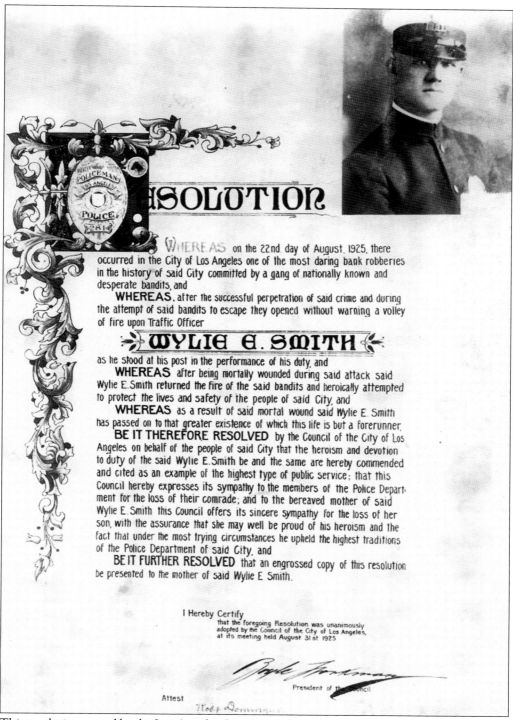

RESOLUTION

WHEREAS on the 22nd day of August, 1925, there occurred in the City of Los Angeles one of the most daring bank robberies in the history of said City committed by a gang of nationally known and desperate bandits, and

WHEREAS, after the successful perpetration of said crime and during the attempt of said bandits to escape they opened without warning a volley of fire upon Traffic Officer

WYLIE E. SMITH

as he stood at his post in the performance of his duty, and

WHEREAS after being mortally wounded during said attack said Wylie E. Smith returned the fire of the said bandits and heroically attempted to protect the lives and safety of the people of said City, and

WHEREAS as a result of said mortal wound said Wylie E. Smith has passed on to that greater existence of which this life is but a forerunner,

BE IT THEREFORE RESOLVED by the Council of the City of Los Angeles on behalf of the people of said City that the heroism and devotion to duty of the said Wylie E. Smith be and the same are hereby commended and cited as an example of the highest type of public service; that this Council hereby expresses its sympathy to the members of the Police Department for the loss of their comrade; and to the bereaved mother of said Wylie E. Smith this Council offers its sincere sympathy for the loss of her son, with the assurance that she may well be proud of his heroism and the fact that under the most trying circumstances he upheld the highest traditions of the Police Department of said City, and

BE IT FURTHER RESOLVED that an engrossed copy of this resolution be presented to the mother of said Wylie E. Smith.

I Hereby Certify
that the foregoing Resolution was unanimously adopted by the Council of the City of Los Angeles, at its meeting held August 31st 1925

President of the Council

Attest

This resolution passed by the Los Angeles City Council regarding Officer Wylie E. Smith in 1925 speaks for itself. Since 1907, nearly 200 police officers have been killed in the line of duty.

In 1923, this officer was responsible for keeping traffic flowing at Hollywood and Cahuenga Boulevards. Looking at those tracks and his location, it would take nerves of steel to stand still when an eastbound and westbound streetcar happened to pass each other right at that point.

Formed in 1923 under Chief August Vollmer, the Crime Crushers were a part of a 300-officer mobile detail that was deployed to saturate targeted high-crime areas. Criminals were arrested, property recovered, and crime reduced. In addition to mobile crime response, the Crime Crushers also attacked organized crime. Chief Vollmer warned gangsters that many of them "would die" if they remained in Los Angeles.

In trying to draw attention to his advertising gimmick for a Chandler motor car dealer in 1929, this Harpo Marx look-alike succeeded only in gaining the attention of a disapproving LAPD officer. Considering that contraption, the ticket must be for parking and not for speed.

A young LAPD officer has his hands full (around 1927) as he simultaneously attempts to hold back traffic and the lady on the left while trying to answer the question being posed to him by the other.

Fairly late on a sunny afternoon in 1927, judging by the shadows, Hollywood Division gathered for an inspection on pepper tree-lined Vine Street just north of Hollywood Boulevard. Their station at that time was three blocks west on Cahuenga Boulevard, but apparently this thoroughfare lent itself to quieter surroundings. The building under construction was the new U.S. post office, which in later years became a popular cafeteria. Holding an inspection at this same location today would be hard to imagine as it is one of the most famous and busiest intersections in the city.

In 1927, these four officers became fairly well-known for their barbershop harmony. They appeared on local radio and were undoubtedly a plus for the department's public relations. If the officer on the right is the leader, he is using an intimidating method to keep the other three from hitting any sour notes.

This Los Angeles street is well protected as both motorcycle and regular patrolmen line up for inspection, sometime in the late 1920s. The small uniformed fellow at left is most likely the young "mascot" of the division. While unidentified, a similar little boy appears in a few other photographs and is referred to in that way.

An incredibly happy group of motorcycle officers virtually covers a truck sometime in the late 1920s. The photograph carries no explanation, but they seem to be having such fun that one wishes you could step into the picture and join in.

Rarely do you see an auto made by Pierce Arrow anymore, much less an ambulance from that long defunct company. In 1927, the police provided the city's ambulance service, and pictured here are Charles "Charlie" Whitenend, the department's chief nurse, along with a police officer who was the driver and, presumably, Charlie's protection, just in case.

In 1927, this LAPD officer directing traffic at Broadway and West Eleventh Street took time out for a "tea break," served up by an appreciative waitress in a nearby restaurant. Officers at fixed post positions, such as this one, or on regular foot beats, get to know and be known by the people who work and live in the neighborhood. That stability-of-assignment premise was used as the basis for the innovative Basic Car Plan, initiated by the department around 1970. The plan emphasized keeping the same team of officers assigned to a radio car district for an extended period, thereby increasing their familiarity with the area and communication between them and the public regarding criminal activity. (Courtesy Security Pacific Collection, Los Angeles Public Library.)

The police boat located at the Los Angeles Harbor was periodically used to dispose of contraband. In this photograph, taken around 1920, a team of uniformed officers and detectives prepare for the three-mile trip to perform that task.

In this photograph taken off the stern of the patrol boat about 1930, the disposal of contraband firearms in the ocean is carried out and doesn't look like bad duty at all, particularly on a hot Southern California summer day.

The police patrol boat, here cutting across Los Angeles Harbor, was part of Harbor Division. This sea-going patrol unit monitored potential criminal activity for many years. The combined Los Angeles/Long Beach harbors became the busiest import/export spot in the United States. At that time, the Los Angeles Harbor Department, a separate agency of the city, was given the responsibility for law enforcement in the Port of Los Angeles. Its several patrol boats now monitor the harbor.

A group of LAPD officers prepare for work in Hollywood in the late 1920s. Note the special billing for "Police Woman" sharing the transom window with the sign for the Detective Bureau.

In 1936, two policemen stand in the doorway at the Wilshire police station. This station at 4526 West Pico Boulevard was built in 1925 but was vacated and demolished in 1974, when a new and larger facility was constructed on Venice Boulevard. (Courtesy Security Pacific Collection, Los Angeles Public Library.)

BASEBALL GAME JUNE 22 1929 BENEFIT DUNBAR HOSPITAL L.A. POLICE VS. L.A. DOCTORS
In Foreground: James E. Davis, Chief of Police & H.A. Hoger, Capt. Newton Division   Prbs. by Chief James F. Davis

The Newton Street Lawmen, a team comprised of African-American Los Angeles police officers assigned to the department's Newton Street Division in the 1920s and 1930s, played baseball against both amateur black and professional Negro League ball clubs to raise money for charities. This photograph featuring Chief James E. Davis was taken before a game against the Medicos, a team of local doctors, dentists and other medical professionals, to benefit the Dunbar Hospital. The Lawmen won this contest, 22-15.

In this late 1920s "gag shot," Officer Joe Dircks poses astride a small donkey while writing a citation. A portion of his actual mode of transportation is shown at left. How this photograph came to be staged is unknown, but Officer Joe seems to be getting a kick out of it. Joining the department in 1923, Dircks went on to a long and noteworthy career as a shooting instructor and subsequently rose to the rank of lieutenant at the Police Academy. He was also a member of the widely known LAPD Shooting Team, lived well into his 90s, and was a frequent visitor at the academy long after his well-earned retirement.

Eager motor officers line up in the early 1930s in front of the new city hall on Spring Street. On their front fenders are signs providing full accreditation in case someone doubts who the riders are.

The department's all-female color guard poses on the steps of city hall, *c.* 1950. Pictured, from left to right, are Sgt. Kay Sheldon, Sgt. Mary Galton, and Officer Dottie Doir.

L.A. POLICE MOTORCYCLE DRILL TEAM, LT. JACK LYONS. Nov. 11. 1932

One of the department's early motorcycle drill teams, under the supervision of Lt. Jack Lyons, has its picture taken in 1932.

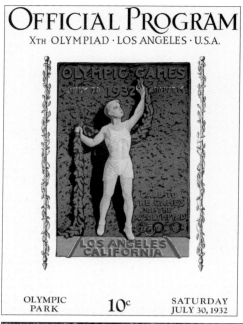

OFFICIAL PROGRAM
Xth OLYMPIAD · LOS ANGELES · U.S.A.

OLYMPIC PARK   **10ᶜ**   SATURDAY JULY 30, 1932

Despite the Depression era, the 1932 Olympics in Los Angeles actually turned a $1.3 million profit and left behind recreational facilities for future use. Contributing to the safety and success of the Olympic Games were 800 police officers under the command of Chief Roy Steckel. This is the cover of the Official Program. In 1984, despite severe cutbacks in resources, it was Chief Daryl Gates's responsibility to prepare the LAPD for the upcoming Games of the 23rd Olympiad in Los Angeles. Requiring protection were 1.5 million anticipated spectators, 12,000 athletes, 10,000 members of the media, and 3,000 game officials—all of whom simultaneously converged on Los Angeles. The successful security provided for the Olympic Games helped cement the LAPD's reputation as one of the finest police departments in the world.

With guns drawn and pointed skyward, motorcycle officers prepare for inspection on a sunny morning in 1923. These were still the days when inspections could take place on a major Los Angeles thoroughfare, replete with streetcar tracks, and not create a traffic jam.

Several annual uniform inspections in the 1930s were held in the Los Angeles Memorial Coliseum and also involved an exhibition of the department's prowess in certain areas such as motorcycle stunts, pursuit driving, self-defense, etc. Here a dog stands on the back of a police officer's bike holding two flags in his mouth while simultaneously checking for pursuers. (Courtesy Security Pacific Collection, Los Angeles Public Library.)

Another demonstration of the department's crime-fighting techniques is shown in this photograph taken at the Coliseum following an annual inspection. Here the suspicious looking individual in the cap is having his gun hand controlled by the canine partner of the officer who has taken cover at the side of the car. (Courtesy Security Pacific Collection, Los Angeles Public Library.)

Two policemen stand in the doorway of LAPD's Seventy-seventh Street Station, which was located at 235 West Seventy-seventh Street, about 1936. Built in 1925 and significantly remodeled in the 1960s, this station was finally demolished in the mid-1990s. Housed in temporary quarters nearby, since the old plot was being used to construct the new and larger station, the officers finally moved into their new high-tech station in 1997. Confusingly, the new building was turned to face an adjacent street, which results in the address of the Seventy-seventh Street station now being at 7600 South Broadway. (Courtesy Security Pacific Collection, Los Angeles Public Library.)

In 1936, four cars are backed to the curb in front of the West Los Angeles police station, apparently ready for a fast start. This building located at 1653 Purdue Avenue was first opened in 1927 with officers occupying several other temporary quarters for the 10 years prior to that. In the mid-1970s, a new station was constructed one block west at 1663 Butler Avenue, and this classic but undersized building was demolished for additional parking. (Courtesy Security Pacific Collection, Los Angeles Public Library.)

In 1937, the Los Angeles Police Revolver and Athletic Club (LAPRAAC) published a yearbook entitled "The Guardian" that covered much of the department's history up to that point, plus details regarding each of the units and divisions, including rosters of personnel that made up the LAPD. Cleverly, the editor arranged for each of the geographic divisions to be posed in a location representative of the area it covered. Two samples of those photographs are shown on this page. Hollywood Division is fittingly lined up on the back lot of a movie studio, and Hollenbeck Division officers decorate a picturesque bridge over the lake in Hollenbeck Park.

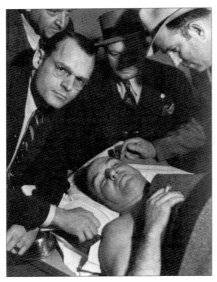

In 1937, Mayor Frank Shaw and Chief James Davis announced that organized crime and protected vice interests were almost nonexistent in Los Angeles. The statement propelled Clifford E. Clinton, a restaurant owner, to national prominence as a civic reformer. The son of Salvation Army missionaries, Clinton was well known in Los Angeles, and in 1937 was appointed to the grand jury. Clinton announced that rampant vice still existed in Los Angeles, and he formed the "Citizens Independent Vice Investigation Committee" (CIVIC). Mayor Shaw struck back. A dynamite explosion nearly destroyed Clinton's residence. Fortunately, no one was hurt. Clinton's crusade could well have failed had not someone tried to murder Harry Raymond, an ex-LAPD cop employed by CIVIC to investigate corruption in the mayor's office. One day, while Raymond was attempting to start his car, a bomb exploded, badly wounding him. Raymond is pictured here with Clinton. The ensuing investigation revealed that Capt. Earl Kynette of the Police Intelligence Division wired the car's explosives. Kynette was tried, convicted, and sentenced to 10 years in San Quentin. The investigation also exposed the widespread corruption in the Shaw Administration. In September 1938, Shaw became the first mayor in the nation to be recalled. Clinton's determination and fearlessness were instrumental in cleaning up Los Angeles. Clifton's, Clinton's restaurant, continues to operate in downtown L.A.

The Radical Squad, later known as The Red Squad, was formed in the 1930s to help "disrupt communist activities," and included the investigation and control of other radical doings, strikes, and riots, and denial of permits for protest marches. This photograph is of Capt. William "Red" Hynes and his Red Squad in action, c. 1930. Red had the support of such groups as the chamber of commerce, county grand jury, mayor, city council and much of the media, including the Los Angeles Times. These people praised the squad's raids on "subversive" organizations.

In 1939, these officers assigned to the mounted patrol show off their riding skills. It appears, for lack of a better explanation, they were shy one horse that day.

Three uniformed LAPD officers grace the cover of this 1948 program from the 14th Annual Los Angeles Police Show celebrating California's centennial. The annual police shows were star-studded events featuring the talents of police officers and Hollywood entertainers to raise money for various youth groups. The Annual Police Show began in 1934 and lasted until the late 1950s.

Sometime in the 1940s, two sharp-eyed motorcycle officers scan an intersection for errant drivers.

This appears to be one of the first major traffic accidents involving streetcars in Los Angeles. The unhappy victims in the vehicle appear to be unhurt and may be very familiar to you. Need a hint? You probably have to be over 40 to recognize them.

The "Black Dahlia" is one of the most famous unsolved murders in America. Numerous books, articles, and films have perpetuated the public's fascination with the case. It derived its name from the victim's dyed, jet-black hair and her habit of wearing black clothing. Elizabeth Short, shown in the photograph at right, was just 22 when, after drifting around the country and becoming involved with several men, she disappeared from a downtown Los Angeles street in January 1947. Five days later, her nude, mutilated body, severed at the waist, was found in a vacant lot shown in the photograph below. Some items from her purse, including her Social Security card, birth certificate, and personal letters were mailed to a local newspaper with an unfulfilled promise of a follow-up letter containing more information. The sender was never traced. Literally dozens of theories and hundreds of leads were investigated. Countless false confessions complicated the case, which remains an open investigation with LAPD's Homicide Division. No one was ever formally charged. (Courtesy LAPD™ Scientific Investigation Division.)

Employee morale has always been considered important to the LAPD administration, and various techniques to sample it have been created through the years. This rather direct, but probably effective, method was used in the Central police station around 1949. (Courtesy Marc Wanamaker.)

This very solid-looking Central Station was built in 1896 on the southeast corner of First and Hill Streets. At the time of the station's opening, the department consisted of 93 officers, including a matron. Twenty-three of those were detectives, leaving a total of 69 officers for patrol.

In the early 1950s, Officer Charles Howe posed for the photograph shown on the wall, around which the department placed specifications as to the proper wearing of the uniform. A large framed version of it graced the walls in locker rooms for many years so that officers could check themselves prior to inspection, as this sergeant is doing. The cross strap was discontinued in late 1957 when it was determined that too many suspects used it as a convenient "handle" when resisting arrest.

In April 1948, an LAPD motorcycle vanguard clears the way for a major parade as they head south on Broadway. This view reflects a downtown long before suburban malls and multiplex cinemas, when streetcars still brought Angelenos into the heart of the city to visit the major department stores and where huge movie palaces played first-run features.

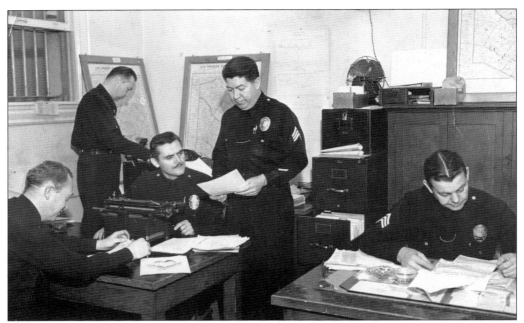

The incredible number of man-hours saved by computers that can analyze crime trends and track suspects is nowhere more evident than in this 1950 shot of the Central Division Analytical Unit, when brainpower was used to do it all. Shown are Ken Cochran, Ted Meier, Chet Poole, Joe Jackson, and Sgt. Gil Burgoyne (standing).

"Aw, give us a break, officer. We're just having a little fun," is what the young man on the left is probably telling Valley Division Officer Manning. Meanwhile, Manning's partner, Officer Weston, checks the license on his buddy. In 1948, when this picture was taken, the entire San Fernando Valley, consisting of over 200 square miles, was being handled by one police division. The formerly rural expanse now has six police divisions to serve more than one million residents.

An accident investigation officer prepares his report on a driver who obviously came to a stop as the sign commanded, but took the sign and what looks like a signal with him in the process. The license plate appears to date this photograph at about 1949.

Whenever W. C. Fields heard a joke he didn't like, he would jokingly yell for a policeman. While making, *Never Give a Sucker an Even Break* at Universal Studios in 1941, his director Edward Cline, who was a good friend of the LAPD chief, called Fields's bluff and out stepped Chief Clemence Horrall. Fields at first thought it was just a gag and not a real cop, but the all powerful LAPD badge convinced him otherwise. (Courtesy Marc Wanamaker.)

Holding an unusual radio microphone, an LAPD radio car officer in the late 1940s puts out a broadcast.

Prior to moving to the new Police Administration Building in 1955, the master control room for communications was located in city hall. It was in operation from about 1943 until the move. The Federal Communications Commission required it to be identified, and its call letters were KGPL, which officers were supposed to repeat after each transmission. This later changed to KMA 367 and remained that for several years. This late-1940s photograph gives the appearance of a commercial broadcast booth, complete with "quiet" signs.

Female officers practice their shooting skills in 1948. In the background at the railing on the left is the city's first female police commissioner, Mrs. Curtis S. Albro, standing next to Chief Clemence B. Horrall.

Fortunate is the man who loves his work. The smile on this motorcycle officer in the 1940s as he sits astride his Harley strongly indicates his love of duty.

A shooting demonstration by the world-famous LAPD pistol team is conducted at the police academy about 1950. Their proficiency is certainly trusted by the two officers holding the chalk in their mouths.

The dashboard and steering wheel in this 1948 Ford seem oddly fancy for a police cruiser, but the new 35-megahertz radio is actually the intended focal point of the photograph. It may not compare with today's sophisticated communications, but at the time it was a giant leap forward in technology.

This late-1940s photograph shows a couple of L.A.'s finest trying hard to live up to the department's motto, "To Protect and to Serve."

The motorcycle squad backs its bikes to the curb around 1950 for inspection in front of the old Traffic Division building on Figueroa Street. The opening of the new police headquarters building in 1955 allowed for the centralization of many of the divisions that were scattered around the downtown area due to lack of space.

These two officers in the 1950s were assigned to the Women's Jail, one of the few assignments that sworn Los Angeles policewomen were allowed to work prior to the 1970s, when they were allowed to become field-certified for patrol and other duties. Today women are represented in virtually every aspect of American law enforcement. The woman performing the pat-down search is policewoman Roberta Riddick who became one of the department's first black female police sergeants. Policewoman Theda Keeler, behind the counter, stands ready to do the paperwork.

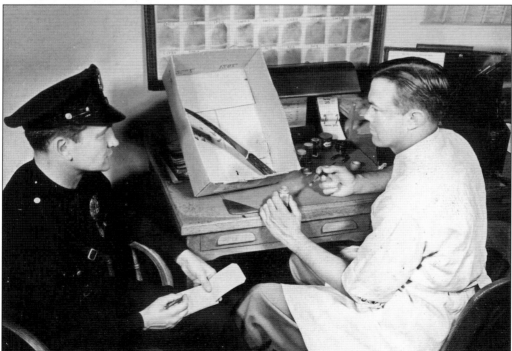

This police officer, accompanied by a civilian Scientific Investigation Division fingerprint expert, is looking over a murder weapon, c. 1940. The role of civilian employees in the LAPD has been critical to its success by filling non-field positions, thereby freeing officers for front-line duties. Civilians are found throughout the department in positions such as records, personnel, jail, and many others. They not only fill basic positions but supervisory and command positions as well.

Through the years, thousands of full-time LAPD police officers have pursued parallel, part-time careers in armed forces reserve programs. In this 1950 "special effect" cover from the monthly department news magazine, Officer D. K. Jones of Central Division checks himself in the mirror wearing his other career uniform, reflecting his role as a 1st lieutenant and commander of Headquarters Company, 2nd Battalion, 160th Infantry.

In 1948, Pres. Harry S. Truman, by executive action, ordered all government employees to take loyalty oaths and declare they were not, nor ever had been, communists. The "Red Scare" era also included congressional hearings on the politics of Hollywood personalities. Every member of the LAPD complied with Truman's order. This December 13, 1948 photograph shows a large group of them taking the oath outside city hall. (Courtesy *Herald-Examiner* Collection, Los Angeles Public Library.)

This silhouette of a 1950s officer starting his beat reflects a new order of police work in Los Angeles. Parker had just become chief, and from now on an officer could do his job honestly and professionally without political interference and without regard to "pull" or "connections." As quick as Parker was to fire a dishonest officer, he was just as quick to defend an honorable officer doing his job.

Four

PROFESSIONALISM AND A NEW TRADITION

1950–1970

A proud, 1957 graduating class strides toward the parade field and the ceremony that completes their basic training. The academy's verdant grounds and picturesque buildings are the result of a unique cooperative between the City of Los Angeles and the officer-owned and -run Revolver and Athletic Club. Initially started as a shooting range in a remote canyon in the mid-1920s, the club added buildings constructed for the 1932 Olympic Games, then enlarged and improved it all through officers' labor and personal contributions. The city later made a deal to begin training its police officers at that location around 1935. That arrangement continues to this day.

Two officers enter Parker Center, the police administration building downtown at 150 North Los Angeles Street. To the officers' right on the wall is a controversial sculpture representing "the family."

A passing press photographer snapped this 1954 picture on South Olive Street of a traffic officer in command of two kneeling men suspected of a crime that has been lost to history. The casual gentleman passing on the right seemed to be amazingly unperturbed by the action.

Jack Webb, the creator and star of *Dragnet*, is visited on location by Lt. Dan Cooke, longtime press relations representative for LAPD. Cooke was assigned to the Public Affairs Division and worked closely with many feature film and television productions throughout the 1960s and 1970s. He ensured that the productions received the appropriate technical advice and complied with previously agreed upon conditions if they were going to represent the Los Angeles Police Department. The man at right is an executive with Webb's Mark VII productions.

Chief Parker and Jack Webb chat on the *Dragnet* set in 1963. Upon becoming chief in 1950, one of Parker's inheritances was Webb, who wanted to produce a truly realistic radio show about the LAPD. Thus, *Dragnet* was born. When Webb wanted to produce a weekly television series patterned after the radio show, Parker was suspicious. But he gave his tentative approval after Webb convinced him of his sincerity and desire to portray the real daily life of a Los Angeles police detective sergeant. The first televised version of *Dragnet* appeared in December 1951. *Dragnet* did more to develop public relations and promote the professional image Parker sought than any other department program. Webb's contribution to the LAPD did not end with *Dragnet*. He created the Police Academy Trust Fund and pledged a percentage of his profits from *Dragnet* and *Adam 12* to enable the academy to make major capital improvements.

Officers Pete Malloy and Jim Reed of the TV series *Adam 12*, played by Martin Milner and Kent McCord, go into action. This photograph appeared on the cover of the department's Beat Magazine in the early 1970s. For seven seasons starting in 1968, fans of the LAPD sat down every week to catch a glimpse of these patrol officers as they chased bad guys and gals in Los Angeles.

LOS ANGELES POLICE   THE BEAT

Producer Jack Webb and Kent McCord engage in a planning session for an *Adam 12* production. Both men had a profound and positive influence on the image of the LAPD, resulting in young people from all over the world coming to join the department to be one of "the best."

With the growth of freeways crisscrossing Los Angeles, specialized units were needed to effectively handle the traffic problems. More powerful vehicles and calibrated speedometers upon which to base enforcement and prosecution were needed. In this photograph, special clocking devices are shown in a roll-bar equipped "FT" unit along with a helmeted accident investigation officer wearing a shoulder harness. All of these were very "state of the art" in the late 1950s and early 1960s. In 1964, LAPD relinquished freeway enforcement to the California Highway Patrol.

The department's Parking and Intersection Control Division (PIC) consisted of sworn officers as the primary enforcers issuing parking citations and directing traffic at strategic intersections. With the creation of a separate city Traffic Department in the 1970s, responsibility was transferred to civilian traffic officers, freeing hundreds of police officers for other assignments. This PIC officer controlling traffic in 1954 is narrowly missed by a streetcar, which conveniently displays an LAPD recruiting poster.

Chief of Police William H. Parker smiles broadly as he meets Gen. Douglas McArthur.

HEADLINER OF THE YEAR

On March 30, 1966, Chief Parker Was Honored by the Los Angeles Press Club at the Biltmore Bowl as Headliner of the Year. Accompanying Him to His Table Are Marti Barris (Miss Press Club '66) and Actress Luana Patten.

Chief Parker again issues one of his rare smiles while attending a dinner in his honor just a few months before his death.

In 1959, two LAPD mounted officers work the Hansen Dam area of Foothill Division. The mounted unit has proven invaluable in crowd control, search and rescue, and more. Officer Dale Rickards writes the citation and the mounted officer is Jeff Squires.

Officers are required to meet a minimum qualifying score in order to maintain their skills at the firing range. However, that never was a difficult task for Lt. Al Strand, a member of the department's exhibition shooting team. Here he is performing a trick shot with the help of a mirror.

Two LAPD officers deal with a lost child, *c.* 1960. The young man may be happy with his ice cream cone, but he's not so sure about the "ticket" being written by the policewoman.

Chief Parker and Capt. Sid Barth inspect the policewomen's graduating class at the Los Angeles Police Academy, *c.* 1960.

The July 1966 funeral procession for Chief Parker is shown shortly after leaving St. Vibiana's Cathedral downtown. Parker was buried amid an overwhelming display of respect from his admirers. Cardinal James Francis McIntyre presided over the Requiem Mass, attended by an overflow crowd of 3,500 people, including Gov. Edmund Brown, gubernatorial nominee Ronald Reagan, and hundreds of law enforcement officers—60 police chiefs among them. The post-Mass procession of 280 automobiles and 300 motorcycles with red lights glowing wound its way from downtown to the San Fernando Valley for graveside services. The procession was routed past the Police Administration Building on Los Angeles Street, on the left side of the photograph. It took 25 minutes for the huge cortege to pass, with dozens of officers saluting the hearse. No better prototype for the peace officer exists than the life of William H. Parker.

The Police Administration Building, opened in 1955, was rededicated and renamed Parker Center after Chief Parker's death in 1966. This photograph was taken at the dedication ceremony. In the foreground are several police commissioners, Mayor Sam Yorty, Mrs. Helen Parker, and Gladys Parker, the chief's mother. Behind Helen Parker are Jack Webb and Chief Tom Reddin.

The smiling officer in this obviously staged photograph does not seem too concerned about getting his hand freed from the mouth of this playful pooch. We are left to guess what the nature of his call will be.

Accident investigators see more than their share of tragedy, and this severe crash illustrates it. One can only hope that the white shirted man talking with the officer is one of those lucky drivers who periodically come through something as horrific as this without a scratch.

With flashlight in hand, two officers exit the front doors of the Seventy-seventh Street Police Station, equipped to patrol and investigate crimes on the streets of South Los Angeles in the 1950s.

During a record rainfall in 1955, Officer W. Davison is high and (relatively) dry as he directs traffic at Seventh and Grand. Police officers are known for their creativity during unusual situations and this officer obviously is no exception.

This precious young lady is proof positive that you can never start too early in preparations to become an LAPD officer!

Obviously staged for public relations, this photograph nevertheless represents a common activity for Los Angeles police officers. The LAPD must remain one of the most proactive police departments in the world in order to effectively police a 460-square-mile city of nearly four million people with fewer than 9,000 officers.

In the fall of 1973, the first "unisex" program was initiated at the academy. This "coed" training eliminated the practice of having periodic policewomen classes with significantly modified requirements, which allowed women to only attain the rank of sergeant. They could also only supervise other women officers, and were limited in their duties to such things as working Juvenile Division, the Women's Jail, and certain detective and vice assignments. This photograph of the policewomen class of May 1967 shows the uniform of that era as modeled by, from left to right, Cecilia Hernandez-Dominguez, Gail Ryan, Shilah Johnson, Rita Knecht, Pat Berry Russell, Gaylene Edgerton, Angela Cimino Morris, Roberta Shouse Minor, and Charlene Lucas Daniel.

A grateful Pres. Dwight D. Eisenhower thanks a squad of LAPD motor officers for providing his escort during his visit to the Los Angeles Police Academy in the 1950s.

On December 14, 1963, a leak at a Baldwin Hills reservoir broke through the external wall. Efforts to halt the flow were outstripped by the pressure of more than 259 million gallons of water. At 2:00 p.m., urgent evacuations began, since no one could say when the reservoir wall might collapse. Danger was imminent. Officers ran from door to door, urging residents to leave the path of the impending flood. Within 90 minutes they had carried the warning to every dwelling in the threatened area. Five minutes after evacuation, a 25-foot-wide crevasse opened in the reservoir wall and tons of water swept down the hill. Everything in the water's path was washed away. Building foundations buckled, and homes were reduced to debris. Several officers made heroic rescues of people trapped in their automobiles, which had been swept away like toys by the onrushing flood.

Officer Lee Kirkwood talks to a lost child at Santa Monica Beach in the 1960s.

Having just won the 1960 nomination for president at the Democratic National Convention in Los Angeles, John F. Kennedy heads for his plane at LAX. Leading the group is Sgt. John Hughes, who was in charge of security at the airport. Sergeant Hughes is assisted by uniformed LAPD Officers Smith, Hydinger, and Cooper. Most of the others in the immediate group are Secret Service agents.

These impressive castle-like stone gates mark the entrance to the historic LAPD Police Academy grounds. Legend has it that they were constructed of old ballast stones used in sailing ships that frequented the Port of Los Angeles. The stone walls on each side of the road were constructed during the Depression and consist of concrete slabs removed from city streets and sidewalks. They are intermixed with vertical columns of decorative lava rock. Behind the main academy building is an elaborate cascading waterfall with plants and rambling walkways designed and constructed as part of a Works Progress Administration project. The Police Revolver and Athletic Club, which is in joint tenancy with the City of Los Angeles, often rents out that picturesque area, known as the "Rock Garden," as a backdrop for parties, weddings, and commercial photograph sessions.

In this undated photograph, an all-male police recruit class is frozen in the potentially painful "squat exercise" while still maintaining their straight lines. The bucolic surroundings of the academy athletic field belies the agony that all police trainees, past and present, have experienced there.

The Police Academy's picturesque setting in Chavez Ravine is three miles from downtown Los Angeles. The large building was added to the original 1932 Olympics buildings in the mid-1930s and houses a gymnasium, locker rooms, administrative offices, cafe, and police equipment store. The easily recognizable stone entry gates used in many television shows are located directly in the center of the photograph. Since the early 1960s, Chavez Ravine has also been home to Dodger Stadium, within sight of the academy.

The Combat Range at the Police Academy is one of three main ranges used to teach young police officers not only control of their weapons and accuracy, but tactics that can minimize their exposure to danger. This photograph shows a recruit class practicing the "barricade position," which simulates a situation where an officer can take cover and fire. The tactic includes drawing the gun from the holster and firing several rounds in a matter of seconds while still being scored for accuracy.

The need for on-site coordination by supervisors at unusual occurrences was the genesis for designating a sergeant's car as a command-post vehicle and modifying it accordingly. It was stocked with expanded communications equipment, maps, and other resource materials and designed so that the supervisor could direct an immediate field response from the rear of the vehicle. Such field command posts are generally utilized until the situation is resolved or until the much larger Department Command Post takes over. In this 1961 photograph, a sergeant and another officer demonstrate the dual radios and planning board capabilities resulting from a trunk conversion.

Sitting next to a patrol car to reflect its large size, the Department Command Post contains sophisticated capabilities to handle large or prolonged incidents.

In June 1968, Sirhan Sirhan struggles with his captors immediately after he shot Sen. Robert Kennedy at the Ambassador Hotel. Sirhan's trial dragged on for 14 weeks, but the jury found him guilty of first degree murder. Following the assassination, the department formed a special investigation unit called the "Special Unit Senator." Deputy Chief Robert Houghton and Capt. Hugh Brown headed the new unit with three lieutenants and 45 specially selected Detective Bureau investigators.

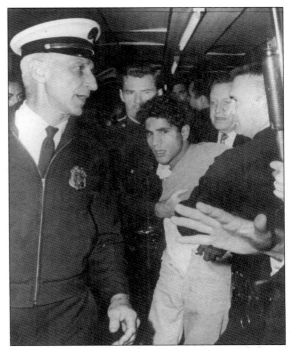

With traffic safety as their primary focus, motorcycle officers move easily through heavy city traffic. However, when an arrest is made, transportation must be handled by the more conventional four-wheeled vehicles. Here in the mid-1950s, a patrol officer on the right accepts an arrested man who is being assisted into the police car by the arresting officers. Normally a second officer sits in the rear seat directly behind the driver to control the arrestee.

This photograph taken during the 1965 Watts Riots shows LAPD officers taking cover after coming under sniper gunfire at an intersection. The Watts Riots lasted six days that August and resulted in 34 deaths, more than 1,000 injuries, over 4,000 arrests, and an estimated $100 million in property damage.

Two officers administer a sobriety test in the early 1950s, asking the motorist to demonstrate balance with his head back and eyes closed as shown by the police officer on the right. The test included having the motorist touch the tip of his nose with the tip of each index finger, with both eyes closed. The individual was then asked to demonstrate balance by walking a line on the pavement placing one foot directly ahead of the other. (Courtesy Security Pacific Collection, Los Angeles Public Library.)

This incredible photograph was taken by a press photographer during the devastating 1961 Bel Air fire, which destroyed literally hundreds of high-priced homes in the mountains of West Los Angeles. Although it has been reproduced countless times, the photograph deserves to be included here. This one picture speaks a thousand words about the courage and personal involvement of police officers when they respond to where the action is.

Just why these motor officers were being rewarded with donuts and coffee in the 1950s is unclear, but undoubtedly it was for a job well done. True to form, the two sergeants have exercised their rank privilege in line.

The police department has always made itself available to the board of education for safety-related training for students. In this staged photograph, a motorcycle officer demonstrates the proper way to signal for a right turn while riding a bicycle.

An early LAPD bomb squad truck's usage is demonstrated by a police officer wearing protective equipment. Fortunately this highly hazardous law enforcement specialty has been made somewhat less dangerous over the years with the advent of electronically controlled robots and more sophisticated personal protective gear for the officers. (Courtesy Security Pacific Collection, Los Angeles Public Library.)

When the Police Administration Building opened in 1955, it housed the most up-to-date communications system of the time. This 1950s photograph is of the complaint board, where the department first received service calls from the public. The handwritten information is placed on the constantly moving conveyor belt, seen here separating the rows of officers, and quickly delivered to the dispatchers in the "horseshoe" seen through the glass partition in the background.

This view of the "horseshoe" reveals the final destination of service messages created by the complaint board. Here they are prioritized by senior officers and passed to one of the radio telephone operators (RTOs) around the circle for broadcast to the assigned unit. Each RTO handled the radio calls for at least one and sometimes two of the geographic divisions. Note the pneumatic tubes in the closest position. These were used for sending handwritten requests for license plate and want and warrant checks to the Records and Identification Division, which was located elsewhere in the building. Responses back to requesting field officers generally took 10 to 30 minutes, depending on tube traffic and the complexity of information requested. Out on the street, officers often felt it took an "eternity" for their information to return.

Dodger Stadium, a popular Los Angeles landmark and home of Dodger baseball, provides the perfect backdrop for three LAPD officers in this 1960s recruitment photograph.

With mountainous Griffith Park being the largest park within a city in the United States, plus the hilly terrain and fire roads that run throughout the city, it was only natural for the department to create a park patrol and equip it with vehicles that could get to difficult places. This early test of an off-road vehicle reflects the start of a program that continues to this day.

This early 1960s photograph of a motorcycle officer using a corner call box to contact the station is nicely juxtaposed against the magnificent Los Angeles City Hall, which forms the focal point of the LAPD badge.

These helmeted Los Angeles police officers face off against a large group of college student protestors. Such scenes were typical during the turbulent 1960s and 1970s.

On March 9, 1963, Hollywood Division plainclothes officers Karl Hettinger and Ian Campbell stopped a Ford coupe containing robbery suspects Gregory Powell and Jimmy Smith. Officer Campbell's gun was taken from him by Powell, causing Hettinger to make the agonizing decision to give up his gun to protect his partner. His decision and the outcome influenced police tactical training. Chronicled by Joseph Wambaugh's best-selling novel, *The Onion Field*, the Campbell/Hettinger saga continued with the officers' kidnappings to a remote field in Bakersfield. There Campbell was shot to death. Hettinger escaped in the confusion, and Powell and Smith separated. However, Powell was quickly picked up by the California Highway Patrol in a stolen car, and Smith later was arrested in a flophouse in Bakersfield. In this photograph taken in a dirt field, the actual moment of Campbell's murder is being reenacted under the supervision of LAPD Homicide Detective Lt. Pierce Brooks, third from left, while Hettinger, second from left, courageously leads the investigating team through the terrifying sequence of events. Detective DeWayne Wolfer, in the white shirt with his hands in the air, acts as the murder victim. In the accompanying photograph, a photographer was present when Smith was handcuffed and lying face down in the filthy hallway of the rooming house where he was hiding out. (Courtesy LAPD™ Scientific Investigation Division.)

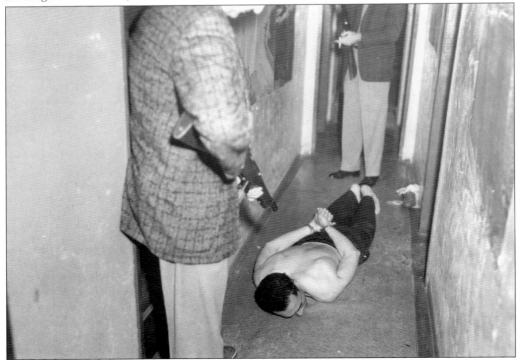

On August 9, 1969, the bodies of actress Sharon Tate and four others were found slaughtered in her Bel Air home. Investigation disclosed that Charles Manson and several of his followers had planned and carried out the murders. The deranged Manson and his so-called "family" were deeply into drug use and had become obsessed with Beatles music and the coming of what Manson referred to as "helter skelter." The following evening, other members of the Manson family randomly selected a house a few miles away and savagely murdered a couple as they returned home. The brutality of these crimes shocked the country and sent a wave of terror throughout the city. All of the suspects were arrested, convicted of first-degree murder, and sentenced to death. The sentences were later commuted to life in prison by the California Supreme Court. These photographs reveal two of the messages that were scrawled, using the victims' blood, on the wall and a refrigerator door at one of the murder scenes. (Courtesy LAPD™ Scientific Investigation Division.)

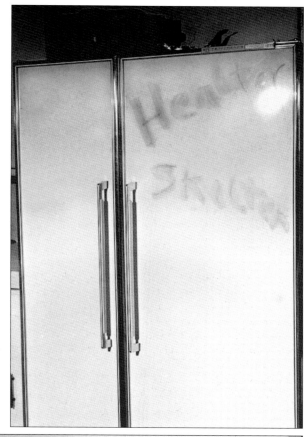

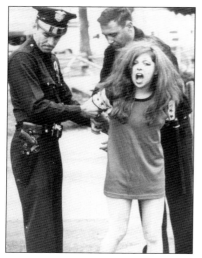

The initial call was "naked lady up a tree" in McArthur Park. With her T-shirt pulled up around her neck, she finally complied with the officers' commands to come down, thus letting gravity provide her modesty. This 1967 photograph reflects her very vocal objection to her arrest for being under the influence of drugs. Retired officer Ernie Anhalt lost his hat during a brief initial struggle with the young lady. The other officer is unidentified.

Apparently unaware of it, this LAPD motor officer receives the "one-finger salute" from two antiwar protestors during one of the countless demonstrations that the department was required to control.

A fire in a South Central Los Angeles neighborhood during the summer of 1967 necessitated that police close down street traffic. Once that was done, the officers at the left in this photograph apparently became a bit distracted by watching the fire department at work and left their squad car to provide bleacher comfort for curious onlookers. (Courtesy Los Angeles Fire Department.)

Five

DEFENDING THE TRADITION

1970–1990

Ed Davis, the 46th chief of the Los Angeles Police Department, inspects the firearms of a class of recruit officers during their graduation ceremony. The time-honored tradition of the recruit officers' final inspection by the chief of police continues to be an important milestone for every officer joining the ranks of L.A.'s finest. Note the officer in the khaki uniform; he is from one of the outside agencies that periodically use the academy for entry-level training.

After Chief Parker's death, the Police Administration Building was renamed Parker Center. Its unbroken facade occasionally provides a "billboard" to promote a department program for press purposes.

Among the longer-lasting of the LAPD's many citizen support groups is the Law Enforcement Explorer program. Until the 1970s unisex training, the Explorer program was limited to males between the ages of 16 and 21 who were interested in law enforcement as a career. The Explorer program adjusted to changing times by admitting females. While affiliated with the Boy Scouts of America, this program operates independently and has provided countless hours of traffic, crowd and other special-event assistance. The training is intensive and culminates in a graduation ceremony much like that of sworn officers. Hundreds of LAPD officers proudly started their careers as Explorers. In this 1971 photograph, West Valley Division Explorer grads have their class picture taken with members of the training staff in dark uniforms, including, from left to right, Lt. Tom Hays, Capt. Al Bauman, Chief of Police Ed Davis, Police Commissioner Elbert Hudson (in dark suit), and Officer Roy Van Wicklin. Standing behind Van Wicklin is Officer George Courtney.

Working in Los Angeles and, in particular, Hollywood, you never know what or whom you'll encounter when issuing a citation or interviewing victims and witnesses. Such was the case for Officer Alan Priest when he received a call regarding a hit-and-run accident. Directed to the set of the film *Boy, Did I Get A Wrong Number*, he found actress Elke Sommer was the victim, whereupon they were joined during the interview by her co-star, Bob Hope. While Alan obediently posed for the cameraman, the two stars fixed their gaze on him.

One of the many popular "cop shows" during the early 1980s with which LAPD acted as a resource was *T. J. Hooker* starring, from left to right, Heather Locklear, Adrian Zmed, and William Shatner. Although location shooting was done around Los Angeles and even at the LAPD Academy on occasion, the show took significant liberties with accepted police tactics for the purpose of dramatic license, and a fictional city was created as their employer. However, the series did reflect much of the challenge and excitement of being a police officer, and was cited by some as stimulating their initial interest in entering law enforcement.

This 1971 photograph was taken at the Tujunga, California, home of retired Chief of Police R. Lee Heath. Chief Heath joined the department in 1904 and was chief from 1924 to 1926. In this picture, he is in his early 90s, being interviewed by coauthor and then-Sgt. Art Sjoquist for a Master's thesis on the history of the LAPD. Also in the photograph to Chief Heath's right is Officer George Wilson, the department's historian. Wilson retired from the department and then was rehired for the position of historian. After two years, the department decided it could not afford a historian, and reassigned Wilson to Communications Division. Wilson quickly retired–again.

Pres. Richard M. Nixon is warmly greeted by a contingency of LAPD motor officers upon his arrival at Los Angeles International Airport.

This LAPD Air Support Division officer enjoys a bird's-eye view of downtown Los Angeles. Starting with one helicopter in 1956, and deployed primarily for traffic patrol of the city's freeway system, the department's Air Support Division is today the largest municipal airborne law enforcement operation in the world. Because of Los Angeles's expansive area, LAPD officers depend upon air support as an around-the-clock patrol tool.

In May 1974, the LAPD caught up with the heavily armed Symbionese Liberation Army (SLA), which was responsible for countless crimes including the kidnapping of heiress Patty Hearst. After appeals to surrender were refused by the barricaded suspects, the police still did not fire a single shot until they faced repeated volleys of automatic gunfire. Despite the firing of over 9,000 rounds in the ensuing battle, no innocent citizen or officer sustained injury from gunfire. A fire subsequently engulfed the house in nine minutes (pictured here). When it subsided, the bodies of six SLA members were recovered. The event was covered live on national television.

Officer Jose Quintero seems to be lost again, and this little girl is taking him back to the police station as she gives him a piece of her mind.

A young LAPD officer kneels down to the street level to interview a crime victim prior to broadcasting the pertinent suspect information to other officers in the area via his mobile ROVER radio. Los Angeles police officers respond to more than 3.3 million calls for service and 1.9 million emergency calls each year. (Courtesy Richard Parmelee.)

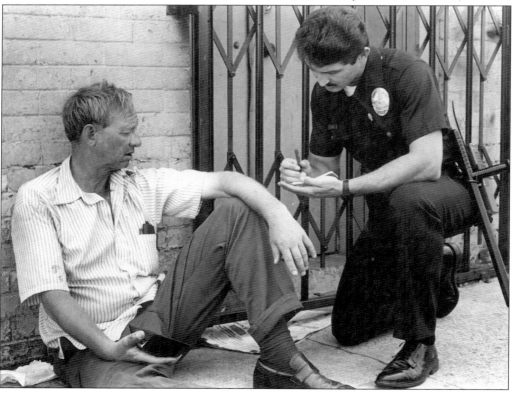

Chief of Police Daryl Gates is accompanied by coauthor Capt. Tom Hays, commanding officer of Training Division, during an inspection at a 1982 recruit graduation. While the ceremony is quite formal and a memorable climax to months of intensive training, it allows the chief to chat with new officers as he reviews the ranks. Typically in all U.S. police departments, new officers received mostly on-the-job training from a senior officer until the mid-1930s. In 1936, the first LAPD academy class graduated. During the 1950s, academy training was generally three months long. In the 1970s, training expanded to the present seven months. It now includes such subjects as conversational Spanish, courtroom testimony, and a myriad of cultural awareness classes designed to deal with the complexities of policing a greatly diverse city.

Standing on the Walk of Fame on Hollywood Boulevard near Vine Street, two of Hollywood's finest check out something that just doesn't look right.

Many talented musicians, including professionals, perform as unpaid volunteers in an LAPD-affiliated concert band, bagpipe band, and mariachi band, all to assist the department. These groups were first formed in 1977 after the city council, for the first time since the band's inception in 1914, cut the budget and refused to support the traditional musical organization formerly composed of police officers. This photograph was taken in the rock garden at the LAPD academy.

Motorcycle officer Jack Velasco assisted in developing a 1984 traffic safety program called the "Blue Knight." The purpose was to reinforce good driving habits by rewarding courteous drivers with such things as coupons for free turkeys and tourist attraction visits. Local news covered this positive program extensively, whereupon Johnny Carson invited Officer Velasco to talk about the program on NBC's *The Tonight Show*.

An impressive phalanx of night-watch motorcycle officers exit the garage of police headquarters to fan out in the city and begin work.

Women have always played an important role in the evolution of the Los Angeles Police Department. Here Chief Daryl Gates poses with sworn members of the department modeling the duty uniforms worn by women dating back to the department's first female law enforcement officer, Alice Stebbins Wells, in 1910. Today a substantial percentage of the department's sworn personnel are women.

When you
need a friend.
The Los Angeles
Police.

This may be a public relations photograph, but the sentiment is genuine.

The original Hard Rock Cafe had nothing to do with the contemporary upscale chain of eateries. Also known as "the working man's bar," the Hard Rock Cafe was no place to take the family. Located on East Fifth Street in downtown Los Angeles, the Hard Rock had its share of shootings and stabbings. Oddly enough, it was right across the street from the Central Police Station. Talk about being able to respond to a call in record time! Here we see Central Division traffic officers, c. 1980, in front of the legendary cafe. Pictured, from left to right, are Officers John Hernandez, James Edge, Joe Wynkoop, Jimmy Hendricks, and Sgt. Richard Parmelee. (Courtesy Richard Parmelee.)

During Pope John Paul II's three-day visit to Los Angeles in 1987, the department played a major role in providing his safety. As he left town, he paused on the roof of the heliport to thank some of the officers assigned to his detail. The Pontiff's legendary warmth is evident as he reaches for the hand of Officer Jack Velasco while Officer Bill Justice, behind him, smiles in appreciation.

Two LAPD officers are close to success as they pursue a couple of fleeing suspects.

Richard Ramirez, 25, his face bruised, is escorted to booking by LAPD detectives at Hollenbeck Division following his capture by enraged East Los Angeles residents on September 1, 1985. Beginning a series of killings, rapes, and vicious beatings less than a year before, Ramirez gained the nickname "Night Stalker" and was the subject of an intense manhunt. Fear and emotions ran high in the city due to his frequent and extremely vicious attacks. Finally identified through witnesses and fingerprints, Ramirez was unaware that his photograph and description were released. A day after the publicity, Ramirez was spotted by a liquor store owner, who shouted his identity to passersby. Ramirez ran, and was pursued and subdued by a growing crowd of angry citizens armed with makeshift weapons. Beaten until police arrived, Ramirez reportedly raised his hands, identified himself as the "Night Stalker," and asked police to protect him. Found guilty of 43 counts, including 13 murders and numerous charges of burglary, sodomy, and rape, he remains on death row awaiting numerous appeals. Informed of his guilt in court, he stated, "Big deal, death always went with the territory. I'll see you at Disneyland." (Courtesy Security Pacific Collection, Los Angeles Public Library.)

"YOU CAN BE ANYTHING. But bored" states the caption across the face of this recruitment booklet, which is certainly true for Los Angeles police officers. As one of the smallest per-capita police departments in the nation, the LAPD is constantly on the move. It's an exciting and proud career being a member of one of the most select and dedicated police organizations in the world.

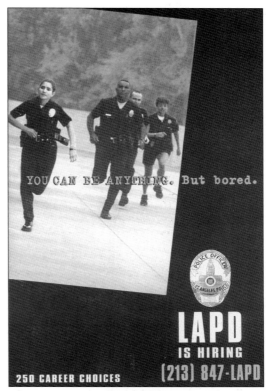

A forensic specialist assigned to the department's Scientific Investigation Division constructs a clay composite in this 1974 photograph. The Los Angeles Police Department opened the nation's first crime lab in 1923 under Chief of Police August Vollmer.

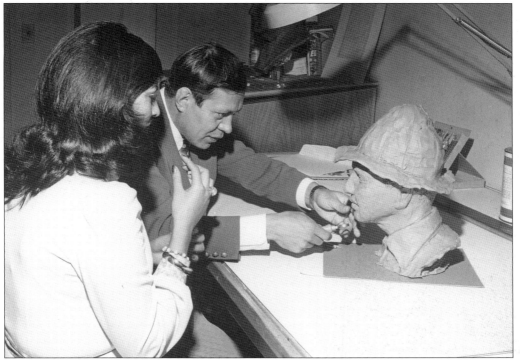

Devonshire Division officers lead children to safety after a crazed gunman opened fire with a 9-mm Uzi automatic pistol at the North Valley Jewish Community Center in Granada Hills in August 1999. The gunman wounded five people, including three children, then shot and

killed a Chatsworth postman before police officers finally captured him. (Courtesy Hans Gutknecht, *Daily News*.)

Roll call is over. Time to go to work!

Six

BADGE OF HONOR, THE LAPD EXPERIENCE

1990–2005

The implementation of the Air Support to Regular Operations (ASTRO) program provided routine air support for ground units. Direct radio communications between air and ground enhanced the success of operations, developing into one of the department's most successful and cost-efficient operations. This 1960s photograph of patrol officers searching a hillside with the aid of an LAPD helicopter is typical of the cooperation between air and ground units. The helicopter's spotlight is capable of literally turning night into day for the officers.

In 1925, Highland Park Division's new station house was opened at 6045 York Boulevard and is the subject of the 1940s photograph above. The building served the department and community for 58 years before the command moved in 1983 to more spacious quarters on San Fernando Road. The York Boulevard structure stood empty and abandoned for nearly 18 years until it was obtained by the Los Angeles Police Historical Society for use as its museum and archival center. It has been significantly restored and hosts both department and community events in addition to retaining and displaying LAPD's colorful past. Below is an artist's conception of the completed future development of the site.

Reflecting the high-tech and dangerous world of modern police work, four K-9 officers and their eager partner position themselves to best advantage at the scene of a call-out. (Courtesy Glenn Grossman.)

April 29, 1992 will forever be remembered as one of the most violent days in the city's history. Hours after the verdicts were read acquitting the four officers who had been on trial for the televised violent confrontation with African American motorist Rodney King, communities throughout the city erupted in violence. This LAPD patrol car responds to the scene of what was only one of hundreds of businesses that were looted and set on fire over a four-day period. Thousands of looters ransacked stores and set fires in a deadly rampage that culminated in 52 lost lives, 2,500-plus injuries, and more than $1 billion in property damage. It was one of the largest incidents of civil unrest in American history. (Courtesy Dennis Sherr.)

One of the most intense shoot-outs in LAPD history occurred on February 28, 1997. The entire nation watched on live television as a gun battle raged between LAPD officers and two heavily armed bank robbers wearing body armor. The gunmen, armed with high-powered automatic assault weapons and thousands of rounds of ammo, were experienced, well trained, and committed criminals who had decided to rob the Bank of America in North Hollywood. Patrol officers spotted the duo entering the bank and called for reinforcements. Inside, the robbers fired weapons and took $300,000 in cash. The duo was surprised to exit and find officers surrounding the bank. Protected by body armor, they began firing armor-piercing bullets and initially had the officers severely outgunned. Officers were successful in obtaining an armored transport vehicle and borrowed assault weapons from a nearby gun store to rescue downed officers and citizens, and hold the robbers at bay until the arrival of SWAT. Heroic officers faced grave danger and initiated rescue after rescue while under a constant barrage of automatic gunfire. Ultimately one gunman ended his own life while the other was shot and killed by SWAT. More than 300 LAPD officers were called to the scene. Ten officers and six citizens were injured. However, the only two lives lost during the shoot-out where those of the bandits. The photograph above shows SWAT officers, from left to right, Sgt. Michael Albanese, Officer P. Weireter, Lt. Tom Runyen, and Sgt. Bob Brannon planning strategy amidst mass confusion.

Officers take cover behind a police car during the North Hollywood shoot-out.

The department's chief from 1997 to 2002 was Bernard Parks, whose most enduring legacy will be the establishment of the Los Angeles Police Foundation in 1998. Through his vision, this foundation's sole purpose is to fund urgently needed police equipment and programs not provided for in the city's budget. Since its inception, millions of dollars have been spent on emergency protective equipment and programs that have helped Los Angeles police officers better protect and serve the city.

Chief of Police Martin H. Pomeroy served as the city's top administrator from May 7 to October 26, 2002. He was presented his official department portrait by executive secretary Mary Helen Ayala and Adjutant Lt. John Thomas. Coming out of retirement to serve as the department's interim chief, he had also served as the department commander during the successful 2000 Democratic National Convention in Los Angeles. Lieutenant Thomas has had the distinction of serving as the aide or adjutant to four LAPD chiefs of police (Bayan Lewis, Bernard Parks, Pomeroy, and William Bratton). Ayala, affectionately known as "MH" throughout the department, has to date served more than 42 years with the LAPD and has become a department "icon."

Two police trainees fix their gaze and their weapons on an imaginary suspect as they practice felony control procedures at the police academy under the watchful eyes of instructors. In this case, the two recruit officers are members of a police reserve class—members of the community who supplement the department by volunteering their services a minimum of two shifts per month. First authorized by the city council in 1947, the Reserve Corps has varied in strength over the years and currently is made up of over 650 members. Three levels of qualification are based on length of training, ranging from 795 hours for a Level I officer, who can work independently in the field; 660 hours for a Level II, who can work as a partner with a full-time officer, and 210 hours for a Level III, who generally works such details as desk officer, assistant to detectives, or field reporter. There are also specialist reserves, who have specific talents or skills and are used in that capacity when the need arises. A recent study determined that the combined total hours worked by reserve officers each month is equal to an extra 100 sworn officers. This successful and highly respected adjunct to the department truly reflects the corps' motto, "Twice a Citizen."

The 54th chief of police of the City of Los Angeles is William J. Bratton.

The executive body at the head of the LAPD is the Los Angeles Board of Police Commissioners. Composed of prominent citizens appointed by the mayor, members of the commission are civilians from all walks of life and represent all areas of the city in its policy-making role. The commissioners as this book went to print, from left to right, are (seated) commission president David S. Cunningham III and vice president Alan J. Skobin; (standing) Corina Alarcon, Rick J. Caruso, and Rose Ochi.

Against a modern panorama of downtown Los Angeles skyscrapers, worlds removed from the sleepy pueblo illustrated in the first chapter of this book, three LAPD airships head into an unlimited future for professional law enforcement. (Courtesy Glenn Grossman.)